S0-BWP-703

Words for Our Feelings

*A Concise and Practical Guide
to the Names for the Various
Moods, Emotions, Sensations and Feelings*

Dan Jones, Ph.D.

Published by Mandala Books & Tapes
P.O. Box 5892
Austin, Texas 78763
0-9633927-0-0

Copyright © by Dan Jones 1992. All rights reserved.
No part of this book may be used or reproduced in any
manner whatsoever without permission except in the
case of brief quotations in critical articles or reviews.

CONTENTS

PREFACE

When someone asks us what we're feeling, what do they mean, and how can we answer?

What are these feelings we feel, and where do they come from, and why? Is there a list somewhere that shows what kinds there are and how many? Do we all have the same feelings? Can we do anything about them?

The purpose of this book is to provide clear and accurate information about the language of feeling, with a view toward improving communication and enhancing relationships between friends, lovers, partners, co-workers, and family members.

Its aim is descriptive, not prescriptive. It doesn't tell anyone what to do, but only shows what feelings are and aren't, and what names for feelings exist in the English language. The idea is that if we can just agree on what the words mean, and thus share the same language, we will have made a very large step toward increasing the peace and harmony in our relationships.

Part I surveys and organizes the entire language of feeling. Part II answers questions most often asked about feelings. Part III discusses the possibilities for improving our feelings.

WORDS FOR OUR FEELINGS

If we take a dictionary and run our eyes down all the columns of words while silently repeating, "I feel _____," and we write down all the words that can, according to standard usage, complete that sentence, not even counting phrases or slang or metaphors, we will still have a list of about 2,000 words. With that large a number, no wonder we have so much confusion about what feelings are.

Fortunately, we can reduce the number.

First, we notice that there is a large group of words that describe the stimulus more than the response. For example, "I feel attacked . . . betrayed . . . befriended . . . pampered . . . tied down . . . ." This is a potentially enormous and open-ended category, since there are any number of verbs and quite a few nouns to which we can add "-ed" and say, "I feel that-ed." These words have one foot in the world of stimulus and one foot in the world of response (feeling), but they lean over toward the stimulus world.

Confusing these words with feelings can cause trouble. If I tell you, for example, that I feel hurt or sad or scared or mad, you can't really argue with that because it's just a statement of the fact of my feeling. But if I tell you that I feel "manipulated" or "abused," you can certainly argue about that, because I'm using the camouflage of "feeling" to call you a manipulator or an abuser.

Using these stimulus words to describe feelings can be avoidance, just as sure as the man who, when asked how he feels, says, "Well, I feel like having a beer," or "I feel that you should . . . ."

(Anytime somebody says "that" after "I feel," they're probably changing the subject.)

Dropping all the stimulus terms will reduce our list by about 300 words, so now we have to deal with only 1700 feelings.

Second, there is another class of words that describe not so much a feeling as an action that flows from a feeling. For example, "I feel adventurous . . . talkative . . . promiscuous . . . guarded . . . generous . . . grouchy . . . ." These words, too, have one foot in the world of feeling, and one foot in the world of action, but they lean over into the world of action.

Mostly, they don't do the mischief that stimulus words can do in arguments, and certainly, like stimulus words, they have their uses; but they do cloud our picture of what feelings are. Striking the 300 or so of them pares our list down to a mere 1400 feelings.

Third, although we like to keep a nice distinction between thought and feeling, we still find ourselves completing the sentence, "I feel _____," with words that indicate mental states: either mental acuity, as in "I feel clear . . . clever . . . reflective . . . resolved . . ."; or mental confusion, as in "I feel baffled . . . dazed . . . muddled . . . ."

Chronic intellectualizers, thinking that this is almost their entire vocabulary of feeling, may object to this particular cutting, but we are going to transplant the 200 words for mental states, leaving us with 1200 feelings to go.

All the rest on our list are more nearly feeling words proper, but fortunately we can still do some more pruning. There is a large class of words that describe general moods, non-specific states of overall well-being: "I feel great . . . fine . . . super . . . terrific . . ."; or middling: "I feel OK . . . tolerable . . . decent . . ."; or ill-being: "I feel awful . . . crummy . . . low-down . . . ." These are useful indicators of where we are on the scale, but they don't take us very far inward, and since we are looking for what the specific feelings are, we will set this group aside for now.

In addition to these general terms, we can feel "usual . . . normal . . . typical . . ."; or "unusual . . . strange . . . different . . . ."

There are also words for feeling improved: "I feel recovered . . . transformed . . ."; and worsened: "I feel relapsed . . . regressed . . . ."

Also, changeable: "I feel moody . . . mercurial . . . ."

All of these non-specific words are about 200, and so our list is now half its original size. Only 1000 feelings left.

The chemical culture, in its verbal flourish, has provided us with many a word for feeling chemically altered (hundreds and hundreds, if we had counted phrases like "drunk as a _____"). From our list of just regular words, however — "I feel high . . . stoned . . . sedated . . . etherized . . ." — we can set aside about 40.

Next, there are words that indicate not a feeling of our own, exactly, but more a feeling for the feelings of others: "I feel sympathy . . . empathy . . . ."

These are very important words for highly good and useful states, but since our search is for specific, personal feelings, we are now down to 950.

Our next group is the largest of all. These are words for physical sensations, and there are so many that we will just sketch an outline of them, with a few examples of each, to show the overall picture. Physical sensations can be:

tactile – hot, cold, clammy, itchy

muscular – stiff, wooden, tense
limber, graceful, relaxed

energetic – throbbing, tingling, streaming
impulsive, impetuous, spontaneous

pain/pleasure – sore, achy, bruised
comfortable, sensuous, thrilled
amused, mirthful

sickness/health – queasy, feverish, toxic
well, fit

weak/strong – feeble, impotent
powerful, muscular

energy availability – lazy, dull, listless
alive, vigorous, enthusiastic

arousal or calm – roused, jittery, turbulent
quiet, still, serene

sexual – sexy, romantic, erotic

```
        body size/shape – fat, lean, bloated, gaunt
       body appearance – pretty, ugly, desirable
kinesthetic sensations – sinking, spinning
                         awkward, clumsy
                         graceful, nimble
                         stuck, constipated
```

(We don't say that we "feel" colors, sounds, tastes, and smells, so we have not included these sensations on our list.)

This language of sensation is what we use when we are athletes and dancers and yogis and martial artists, when we are integrated with, or at least aware of our bodies. We do not hear them as much in classrooms or boardrooms or stores and offices. There are about 400 words for physical sensations.

For the remaining 550 words, we will need to remember what we know about stress ("a force that tends to distort a body," says the Dictionary) and we will need a framework. This framework will allow us to see feelings arising both from the total amount of stress, and also from particular kinds of stresses.

First, when there is too little stress, we feel "bored." Boredom can become an excruciating feeling, and we will go to extraordinary lengths to create some excitement in our lives. This accounts for a good deal of the non-approved student activities in some schools, and also for a hefty percentage of romantic relationships. Anything is better than boredom.

But then, on the theory that if some is good, more is better, we pile on the stresses like sugar in coffee, and rush around until we're tired all the time. Chronic weariness is the master key to a Pandora's Box full of ills and illnesses, and especially when added on to chronic, long-term, accumulated stresses, can lead to one or two or more of the following sets of miserable feelings:

TOO LITTLE STRESS → boredom, ennui, tedium

TOO MUCH STRESS
↓

tired — weary, fatigued, exhausted

tense — tight, anxious, nervous
hyper-excited — frantic, panicky, hysterical

coming apart — fragile, fragmented, unraveled
losing boundaries — shapeless, formless

closing down — withdrawn, distant, disconnected

loss of humor — serious, solemn, grim
loss of feeling — apathetic, numb, depressed
loss of hope — hopeless, despairing, desperate

The worst comes when we forget that we are just very, very over-stressed, and we think that these feelings are Reality. We need someone to tell us to rest. We need to ask for some help.

Before we get too dismayed by all these over-stress words, remember that there is a broad area between boredom and exhaustion where the stress level is better suited to human beings.

Let's imagine an environment that is safe and supportive (not too much stress), and also challenging and rewarding (not too little stress). Here are some feeling words that describe this:

ENVIRONMENT (stimulus)	FEELING (response)
SAFE	relaxed, calm
	open, receptive, trusting
SUPPORTIVE	welcome, belonging
	esteemed, worthy, special
	integrated, harmonious, whole
	free, expansive
	grateful, lucky, humble
	attraction, liking, loving
CHALLENGING	interested, alert, curious
	motivated, inspired, eager
	intrigued, entranced
REWARDING	competent, confident

These are the ones we deserve a lot more of. The over- and under-stress words total around 200. The just-right-stress words also total about 200. A nice balance.

We now have about 150 words left on our list. These involve responses to particular kinds of stress. There is the phenomenon of too-sudden stress of any kind, for example, that gives us feelings like "startled... surprised... astonished... shocked . . . ."

But most of these words describe the special cases that cause the most confusion among us — the so-called negative emotions, like anger and fear and sadness. These emotions really should not be in a category different from physical sensations, which we have already eliminated. What could be more physical than tears, laughter, blushing, flushing, trembling, etc.? Still, they are a special class, because they have a special problem with social acceptability: they can bother people. And somehow we get the idea that we should not have them, or at least we should keep them to ourselves. Doctors can tell us forever that repressing them can make us tense, sick, and depressed, but they will not get very far with the millions who are frightened of these emotions, and the millions and millions more who are ashamed of them.

Still, we are all currently living in the midst of an emotional renaissance, and it might be interesting to at least see what these emotions are. They are responses to specific kinds of stresses, and placed in a chart they look like this:

SPECIFIC STRESS (as perceived)	EMOTION
loss; isolation	sadness
threat	fear
deprivation	desire
nastiness	aversion
insult; frustration	anger
blame	guilt
ridicule	shame

Psychologists recently have been distinguishing the emotions by analyzing the facial expressions of infants. Our list, and in general, all the results of our review of language, are lining up pretty well with the observations of the psychologists. This speaks well either for the accuracy of our language or for the language-boundedness of the psychologists.

The remaining words on our list will group themselves into clusters or families around the seven emotions above, and they will fall out on the page according to their degree of intensity. The purpose of the following chart is to show how, at those times when words like "anger... fear..." etc., are too strong or too weak, we have other choices within the same family.

	Slight	Moderate	Intense	Extreme
SADNESS	disappointed wistful regretful*	dejected despondent lonely	sorrowful mournful disconsolate heart-broken	desolated anguished forlorn
FEAR	uneasy worried apprehensive nervous	anxious frightened scared alarmed	dread panic aghast	terror
DESIRE	wishful nostalgic	yearning wanting longing	craving coveting needy possessive	greedy insatiable

AVERSION	dislike disrespect	repugnance disdain	contempt disgust revulsion	abhorrence loathing
ANGER	frustrated annoyed irritated vexed	resentful indignant exasperated	bitter wrathful rancorous	raging furious
GUILT	regretful* sheepish	repentant contrite sorry	remorseful reprehensible	self-hatred self-flagel- lation
SHAME	embarrassed abashed	unworthy chagrined	shamed disgraced	humiliated mortified

* "regretful" can have either one or both meanings, sadness and/or guilt.

We also have words for these feelings when they become chronic. For example:

> a chronically sad person is **melancholy**.
> a chronically ashamed person is **bashful**.
> a chronically angry person is **choleric**.
> a chronically afraid person is **timid**.

Chronic feelings seem to arise from repeated experiences of holding a particular feeling in, until so much of it has accumulated that it forms something like a lens through which we habitually see and think about the world. Chronic feelings also can fade away as we gradually express the accumulated feelings of these old experiences.

It is not unusual to feel more than one feeling at a time, and we even have words for some of the combinations.

> **envy** is resentment and desire.
> **pity** is compassion and sorrow.
> **shyness** is fear and/or shame.
> **dismay** is fear, confusion, and helplessness.

horror is terror and aversion.

hatred is extreme aversion and/or anger.

awe is fear and wonder.

jealousy is desire, fear, anger, sorrow, guilt, and shame, all in one lovely bouquet.

To sum up, then, when someone asks us what we're feeling, they are asking us what levels and kinds of stress we are under, and how we are responding to them. And we can answer them with

stimulus words,

action words,

mental states, or

feeling words.

The feeling words can indicate

general, non-specific moods,

chemically altered states,

empathetic states,

physical sensations,

general stress responses, or

specific stress responses.

All of these classes of words have their uses in the right contexts; none is more "correct" than another. But it helps to know from which class they come, so we don't think that people are telling us about a feeling when they're actually attacking us, or intellectualizing, or being vague, or otherwise avoiding their feelings.

A final word: everything in this book is the same for women and men, gays and straights, people of all ages, all classes, all races and cultures. The conditioning is different and the patterns vary, but not the feelings. Anger is anger, fear is fear, joy is joy, the same for all, all over the world.

QUESTIONS

Are there feelings for which we have no words?

Well, if there were, how could we talk about them?

On the one hand, thousands of years of close observations and verbal inventiveness have given us a very rich vocabulary of feeling words. On the other hand, people who know the language still sometimes grope for words, saying, "It's sort of like this and sort of like that."

The impression this gives is that the world of feeling is perhaps more complex and sophisticated than the world of language, or at least is more unexplored, and that while we surely have words for all of the major varieties of feeling, there are subtle shadings and blends for which we continue to invent new metaphors.

Are there words for feeling nothing at all?

When our bodies are overwhelmed by too much physical or emotional pain, we may go into "shock." We say that we feel "numb . . . frozen . . . paralyzed . . . ." Some people live most of their lives in chronic shock, and never notice because it feels "normal."

Of course, we are "experiencing" numbness, etc., and it is just a matter of focus whether we call this experience feeling or non-feeling. In either case, the remedy is to come out of shock, and recover more active energy patterns.

Are there people who are not capable of having feelings?

Not unless they've had all their nerves and glands removed.

There is, however, the matter of attention. Many people are not ordinarily accustomed to noticing their feelings because their attention has been trained to other areas, like thinking or acting. The feelings are there all along, of course, and anyone can retrain their attention to notice them, in themselves and in others, more and more of the time. Men can be aware of feelings just as well as women. By the same token, women can be aware of thinking and doing just as well as men. We are not necessarily stuck in these thinking/feeling/acting personality "types"; anyone can become skilled in all areas; it's just a matter of where and how we want to train our attention.

Is there a word for feeling too much?

Sometimes we feel more intensely than the actual situation would really call for, and we overreact. This may happen because we are weakened by alcohol, drugs, food allergens, sickness, or tiredness. But more often it comes about because over the years we have accumulated several layers of old, unreleased emotions, and a stimulus comes along and stirs up the whole stew. Before we can think to stop ourselves, we lash out, freeze up, or break down. The word for this is "restimulation."

Another kind of "feeling too much" might be what is called "sentimentality," or maudlin, mawkish mush. This can mean an excess of sadness or sympathy or penitence or romantic endearments.

Of course, what is excessive to one may be the apple-heart-'n'-dumplin'-soul of another, and we seem to use the "sentimental" word labels to sniff at whatever embarrasses us by displaying something less than our own degree of cool, detached, and worldly sophistication. But then, who knows? — tomorrow we may fall in love, and then?

What is an "emotion," and how does it differ from a "feeling"?

A dictionary will tell us that a feeling is a sensation, that a sensation is a perception, a perception is an awareness, an awareness is a knowledge, and a knowledge is an awareness or a perception.

Or, a feeling can mean an affective state, or a sensitivity, or a sensibility, all of which are defined as states of awareness of feeling.

Or, a feeling can mean an emotion, and an emotion can mean either a feeling, or a subjective response; a response is in turn a reaction, and a reaction is an emotional response.

We are not getting very far along.

This is not the fault of the dictionaries. It just shows how words can flow around each other like eddies and currents in the ocean, without giving us much perspective on the ocean itself.

When we look outside of dictionaries, into books by psychologists and therapists, we can find more definitions of "emotion" than there are emotions. They all seem, however, to regard emotions as a sub-species of feeling, and to go with the etymological root of "emotion," which means to move out from, or to stir up. This etymology of stirred-upness would account for why so many of the so-called negative feelings have traditionally been classed as emotions (anger, fear, sorrow, desire, etc.) and why we have classed as emotions so few of the positive feelings, which tend toward peace, serenity, humility, hope, worthiness, and other not-so-stirred-up feelings.

Beyond that, however, there is not a whole lot of agreement about how many of the feelings are "stirred up" enough to qualify them as emotions, and the reader may be as able as anyone to decide. The category can be more confusing than helpful, since the word, "emotion," has just never had a good sense of its own boundaries.

Is "intuition" a feeling or like a feeling?

Etymologically, "intuition" means the same as "insight," and it's a way of knowing rather than of feeling. Like feeling, intuition is an alogical event, but it definitely means something cognitive, and is a sudden, immediate knowing that bypasses the slower process of going through logical steps.

Incidentally, the boundary line between knowing and feeling is not always clearly discernible, and in cases where we are not sure whether we are describing a state of mind or a state of feeling, we have the word, "attitude," which can mean either one or both.

Why is there so much confusion about "anger"?

Because the word is stretched too thin, has to cover too many different kinds of situations. For example, among other things, "anger" can describe:

1) **anger held in.** The person is tense, tight-lipped, jaw-clenched, fist-clenched, smol-

dering. S/he may have been like this for a long time. We wonder how much longer before the big explosion. We don't want to be around for it.

2) **anger expressed destructively.** The person throws the good china at the wall, or yells and makes a fist in our faces, or maybe even hits us. We are hurt and terrified.

3) **anger expressed covertly.** The person is frightened of anger, and so it rarely explodes, but instead it leaks out sideways, coming at us in disguise, often in attempts to hurt us by making us feel guilty or ashamed.

4) **anger mixed with shame at feeling angry,** which leads to denial of the anger, which then finds no outlet, so it explodes inward at ourselves, fueling the voices of judgment, criticism, and guilt, causing depression or self-condemnation.

5) **anger expressed appropriately.** The person goes into another room and twists a towel and growls, or buys some Goodwill china and smashes it out in the garage, or goes off into the woods and throws rocks at trees, or whatever they do best. Afterward, having let off some pressure, they are more relaxed and smiling. We can breathe easier around them now.

6) **anger as a personal ally.** This anger is aimed not at others, but at our own weaknesses, at our own fears, our own guilt and shame, not in a weak, self-critical way that reinforces the weaknesses, but in a strong, I'll-be-damned-if-I'll-live-with-this-stupid-fear/guilt/shame-for-another-single-day kind of way, that moves us out of weakness and into more powerful and meaningful lives. This kind of anger we could use more of.

7) **anger intelligently modulated and channeled not against people but into good causes.** Rightful anger at social injustice or child abuse or environmental abuse is calmly focused on stopping the abuse and re-educating the abusers. When we have this kind of anger, society is grateful to have us around.

When a word carries this many meanings, it's bound to be confusing, and may lead to some theories that sometimes are possibly a little bit one-sided. The word "anger," in its pure sense, appears to mean nothing more than a very powerful personal force that we can train ourselves to use for any sort of purpose. But since, growing up, many of us experienced someone else's anger only when its purpose was negative—to shame us, quieten us, hurt us—we begin to think all anger aims to hurt us. But it is really the purposes of the anger, not the anger itself, that cause our strong negative or positive reactions.

Similar points can be made about the ambiguity of other feeling words. There is useful fear (the startle response, e.g.), and useless fear (chronic worry, e.g.). There is useful guilt ("I need to learn something from this."), and useless guilt ("I'll never learn."). Desire can draw us into ever more destructive addictions; and desire can be for God alone.

There are good and bad pride. With bad pride, physical tension and fear stay in the body, and can be acted out in judging and criticizing others. With good pride, as grows our sense of worth and greatness, so grows in the body a physically relaxing sense of humility and gratitude for the gifts.

Words are slippery, and the feeling words are especially so. Most of them most of the time need descriptive adjectives to be precise.

Can feeling words be misused?

Oh, boy, can they ever.

When someone says, "I'm not mad at you, just disappointed," and you wish you could fall through a hole in the floor, you have just run into a buzz saw of guilt-mongering called "passive aggression," which is common to martyrs and others who just never, never, ever get angry. Such people may also say, "I want only what's best for you, which is that you stop being so selfish."

Angry people may also say, "I feel sorry for you," but there's something about the tone of their voice.

Another kind of example is when The-Man-Who-Never-Cries comes home and finds that his dog has died, and he puts his fist into the wall and says that he's not sad, just mad at a crazy world that allows tragedies to happen.

All of the above possibilities occur because some people are made to feel ashamed or afraid of certain of their emotions, like sadness or anger, and they will do or say anything to hide or avoid them.

There are other kinds of misuses. "I just want to feel comfortable," can mask insatiable greed.

When people think, "That man/woman is too good-looking for me, but this one looks like s/he would be grateful to have me," they may think they're being loving or generous, but they're really caught in a fog of low self-esteem which they're spreading around.

The feeling word most often misused is "love." Two people say, "I love you." One means, "I commit to you body and soul forever and ever." The other means, "At the moment, I'm feeling some pretty warm feelings."

In endless ways, love gets confused with pity, guilt, fear, rescuing, sex, possessiveness, obligation, manipulation, desperate need, passive aggression, overt aggression ("I'm doing this because I love you."), or sexual abuse ("If you love me you'll. . ."). For a madness of sheer confusion of multiple and contradictory meanings that render a word almost without any communicative value at all, until it's defined, "love" is without any rival, the queen of the carnival of verbal confusion.

Some people say that real love is without need, asks nothing in return, puts no conditions on its giving. In this light, the romantic songs that say, "I love you, I need you," offer a flat contradiction, and a very confusing one, too. But then many people like to hear that love is need for fear that they'll never be loved if they're not needed, and so the confusion continues.

Real love, then, would be something like sharing happiness, or giving or teaching or spreading joy or peace or something good, without looking for anything back. Hard to do all the time, but definitely an improvable talent.

There is almost no end to the ways we misuse the feeling words, and a person who wants to truly understand them must also learn to read tone of voice, facial expressions, and body language.

What is "intimacy"?

This word has several different kinds of meanings. Some concern detailed knowledge of a subject, and some concern sexual affairs. But as it pertains to feelings, intimacy means, etymologically, the act of "making known the innermost."

Two people being intimate reveal to each other what has been hidden. Confessions of fears and embarrassments are common in intimacy, as are expressions of love and appreciation. Old wounds can be brought out, and secret desires, anything that has been private and personal, reserved or censored. The secret sides of the self are shown.

Intimacy is an act of trust. It is trusting another with one's feelings, and requires a considerable degree of safety, especially safety from criticism, ridicule, advice-giving, or abandonment. It is the great and general fear of these hurts that makes intimacy such a hard commodity to come by.

What is "commitment"?

Commitment is not a feeling *per se*, but a pledge, or promise, to a course of action, based on feelings like love or desire, and sometimes on feelings like guilt or fear. Obviously, the quality and intensity of the feelings determine the quality and intensity of the commitment.

This is a booby-trapped word, however, since it has so many different applications. We can commit something to memory, or to the flames. There is the commitment of sins and errors. Crimes are committed, and adultery. Murders are committed, and we can be committed to prison or to a mental hospital. In law, "commitment" means to be placed in the charge of a jailer. And in the end, we commit our souls to the Eternal and our bodies to the grave.

So when we consider a commitment to a relationship, we may hear subtle, subconscious echoes of sin, crime, insanity, prison, and death. When this is the case, a person seeking a commitment from another might have an easier time asking for a pledge than for a commitment.

Is there one feeling that is the best one of all, like serenity, or ecstasy, or love, that is the one we should aim for?

There would be too much argument over that one. However, it is possible to feel several feelings at once, and people have reported a high-energy feeling that is simultaneously serene and ecstatic, and also involves feeling

          safe — meaning without fear
  forgiving — meaning without anger
  forgiven — meaning without guilt
     loved — meaning without shame
    loving — meaning without aversion
  fulfilled — meaning without desire
    joyful — meaning without sadness.

Time, in this feeling seems to slow way, way down, and sometimes even disappears, so that there is no sense of hurry and no thought of worry. There is so little pressure in this feeling that our defenses fade away, and we feel a flowing oneness with all the world. If one were going to aim for a particular feeling, it would be hard to argue against this one. It has no name, but we might call it Heaven.

FINDING THE GOOD FEELINGS

The great question in all this is: Are we subject to these feelings or are they subject to us? In other words can we do very much about them? Can we choose how we want to feel?

The emerging answer appears to be a very strong Yes. The ways and means of doing this are very complicated, and a description of them all is beyond the scope of this book. But in general, the Yes is coming from people who are paying increasing attention to matters of rest and exercise, good diet and breathing, meditation and positive imaging, supportive and challenging environments, and, not the least important, releasing physical and emotional tensions. (People who hold in their emotions seem to repeat the same kinds of scenes over and over in their lives, while people who release their emotions in a safe and appropriate way seem to move on to more fulfilling levels of awareness and achievement.)

Part of our difficulty is that we so seldom hear anyone ask us what we want to feel. Instead, people ask, "What are you going to do?" and "How are you going to do it?" Or,

"What do you want to have?" and "How are you going to get it?" Or, "How do you want to look?" The feelings seem incidental to the doings and havings and lookings.

But then so often we end up with things done and things gotten, and looking good, all right, but the feelings feel all wrong. It is a very different approach to ask first, "How do I want to feel?" — useful, for example, or healthy, or peaceful, or loving — and then to build something, find health, create our lives, directly around those feelings.

What we feel appears to depend on the relationship between two forces:

1) our stress level, and
2) our energy level.

The more our energy, the more stress we can handle and still feel strong, healthy, confident, etc. But let our energy level fall even just a little bit below our stress level — wherever that is — and we begin to weaken and tire, and become subject to the less comfortable feelings.

A definition might be: a feeling is the body's response to the relationship between our stress level and our energy level. Stress can be astronomically high, but if energy is higher, we feel the good feelings. Energy can be low, but if stress is lower, we're all right.

This suggests that there are two things we can do to improve our feelings: one, lower the stress level; two, raise the energy level. In real life in the real world, this is in actual practice exactly how things work.

But stress and energy are both complicated phenomena. Stress, for example, includes not only the large, obvious present time stresses, but also the micro stresses of food and air allergens, and also all of the past stresses, still in our bodies, that we have not yet expressed and healed. And energy can come to us from a myriad of sources — fresh, whole foods, clean water and air, good rest and exercise, beauty and order in the environment, adequate income, good friends, loving mates, spiritual nourishments — all of which, not just some, are important. So managing stress and energy is not just a matter of cancelling an appointment and pouring a powder into the orange juice. It takes a very large and ongoing commitment to self-study, and for most people, some professional help and a support group or two.

Those who stay with it, however, are reporting lives increasingly filled with good feelings. As a reminder of what these good feelings are, here is a final chart, an expanded version of the one on page eighteen. It's suggestive, not exhaustive; intended as helpful, not definitive; since words have multiple meanings and personal connotations, make any changes that appeal to you. As a hierarchy, it reads approximately from the bottom up. The classes are not discrete or exclusive, and we can feel many of these at the same time.

SPACE-TIME				
SENSE	free	expansive	vast	eternal
HAPPY	content	cheerful	joyful	blissful
LOVING	considerate	affectionate	devoted	in love
CALM	composed	still	peaceful	serene
TRUSTING	hopeful	optimistic	confident	faithful
APPRECIATIVE	pleased	grateful	humble	reverent
VALUABLE	competent	worthy	admirable	loveable
ENERGETIC	animated	lively	dynamic	electric
HEALTHY	well	fit	sound	whole

People who have not yet overcome a pattern of perfectionism or "never-enoughness" should beware of charts like this one. ("What? Merely content? Is that all?!") If we can just get on the chart, anywhere we are is more than enough.

It helps to remember that these feelings are results, not things to be taken by force or guile. They come because of something else. We have them when we live our lives intelligently and ask for the help we need, becoming aware of and managing our stress and energy levels so that we have the energy to take on more and greater challenges in the work of helping humanity to continue to evolve into higher states of feeling.

It's a long journey, but it's possible, it's safe, it's mostly fun, and we deserve it. Good luck.

MORE ABOUT FEELINGS

Readers interested in pursuing practical approaches to better feelings will find them in the narrative of the author's personal experiences: *The Roller Coaster Kid Finds His Way Home*, available from Mandala Publications in December 1992.

ABOUT THE AUTHOR

Dan Jones, after serving two years in the Marine Corps, earned a Ph.D. in English and taught American Literature and Language for 15 years. He then resigned a tenured professorship in order to travel and search for ways to find health, peace, and happiness, and how to share those ways with others.

A therapist in Austin since 1978, he was featured in John Lee's *The Flying Boy*, and now co-leads with John the P.E.E.R. Program, a training for professional therapists in emotional release work. He has been happily married for 18 years.

WORDS for our FEELINGS

Printed in Goudy typeface on recycled paper

Editor:	Lyman Grant
Advisor:	Bill Stott
Design and Production:	Bill Jeffers
Cover Design:	John Dolley & Bill Jeffers

NOTES

NOTES